This Book Belongs To

_____

This Book Is about My

_____

This Book Was Given to Me By

_____

Remembering My Pet

A Kid's Own Spiritual Workbook for When a Pet Dies

Nechama Liss-Levinson, PhD and
Rev. Molly Phinney Baskette, MDiv

Foreword by Lynn L. Caruso

Walking Together, Finding the Way ®
SKYLIGHT PATHS®
PUBLISHING
Woodstock, Vermont

Remembering My Pet:
A Kid's Own Spiritual Workbook for When a Pet Dies

2007 First Printing
© 2007 by Nechama Liss-Levinson and Molly Phinney Baskette

For information regarding permission to reprint material from this book, please mail or fax your request in writing to SkyLight Paths Publishing, Permissions Department, at the address / fax number listed below, or e-mail your request to permissions@skylightpaths.com.

Grateful acknowledgment is given for permission to use material adapted
from *Blessing the Animals: Prayers and Ceremonies to Celebrate Gods Creatures, Wild and Tame,*
© 2006 by Lynn L. Caruso. Permission granted by SkyLight Paths Publishing, www.skylightpaths.com

Library of Congress Cataloging-in-Publication Data
Liss-Levinson, Nechama.
Remembering my pet : a kids own spiritual workbook for when a
pet dies / Nechama Liss-Levinson & Molly Phinney Baskette.
p. cm.
Includes bibliographical references.
ISBN-13: 978-1-59473-221-8 (hardcover)
ISBN-10: 1-59473-221-3 (hardcover)
1. Pet owners—Psychology—Juvenile literature. 2. Pets—Death—
Psychological aspects—Juvenile literature. 3. Bereavement—
Psychological aspects—Juvenile literature. 4. Children and
animals—Juvenile literature. 5. Children and death—Juvenile
literature. I. Phinney Baskette, Molly, 1970– II. Title.

SF411.47.L57 2007
155.9'37—dc22

2006033869

10 9 8 7 6 5 4 3 2 1
Manufactured in China

SkyLight Paths Publishing is creating a place where people of different spiritual traditions come together for challenge and inspiration, a place where we can help each other understand the mystery that lies at the heart of our existence. SkyLight Paths sees both believers and seekers as a community that increasingly transcends traditional boundaries of religion and denomination—people wanting to learn from each other, *walking together, finding the way.*

Cover design/Illustrations: Jenny Buono

SkyLight Paths, "Walking Together, Finding the Way" and colophon are trademarks of LongHill Partners, Inc., registered in the U.S. Patent and Trademark Office.

Walking Together, Finding the Way ®
Published by SkyLight Paths Publishing
A Division of LongHill Partners, Inc.
Sunset Farm Offices, Route 4, P.O. Box 237
Woodstock, VT 05091
Tel: (802) 457-4000   Fax: (802) 457-4004
www.skylightpaths.com

Contents

In memory of Oreo and Cookie,
our sweet cats who loved Shabbat and Passover.
—NLL

To Shaggy, my first pet-love; The Loo, our current owner;
and Lilith, Feline of the Night, who shared with me the
Worst Christmas Ever.
—MPB

Acknowledgments

At the end of her time here on earth, I had promised our cat, Cookie, that I would write a book about her and her sister, Oreo. With this book I am keeping that promise. When we brought two kittens into our home twenty years ago, we also brought untold joy and love to our two daughters.

Thanks go to my husband, Billy, who dutifully took on the task of changing the litter, feeding the kittens, and removing cat hair from the couches. He is valiant, loyal, and kind, and with children as well as with animals, he is wondrously playful. Thanks to both our editor, Emily Wichland, and our publisher, Stuart M. Matlins, who had the foresight to suggest this book and under whose thoughtful, competent guidance it was brought to fruition. My coauthor Molly Phinney Baskette continually offers an honest approach to a child's reality, along with a sense of humor that makes me smile.

This book is also dedicated to the fish, turtles, and ladybugs of my childhood, and in honor of our newest family member, Lily, our younger daughter's kitten, who was rescued from the wilds and who, in turn, brings us comfort, happiness, and hope for the future.

—NLL

Great thanks go to the following: Nechama Liss-Levinson, the best writing partner a girl could ask for, for the invitation to work on this project; our editor at SkyLight Paths, Emily Wichland, whose cheerful support made the process delightful; and SkyLight Paths' publisher, Stuart M. Matlins, for providing us with this opportunity. I am deeply grateful to my generous husband, Peter, mother-in-law, Sarah, and father, George, for all the Carmen-hugging and Rafe-corralling they did so that I could have time to write. A big meow-out goes to Beckie Hunter and Neil Marsh, who out of long experience with loving and losing pets gave us some terrific new chapter ideas—I admire your palpable tenderness and care for God's other "people"! And, of course, thanks be to God for making my dream come true twice in one year.

—MPB

A Special Foreword for Parents
By Lynn L. Caruso

Some of my earliest childhood memories involve a companion that spoke most clearly with tail and tongue. From his days as a puppy being paraded around in an antique baby carriage, through years as my faithful running partner, we shared a close bond. And yet at the end of his life, when we made the painful decision to end his suffering, there was no closure. This companion, who had spent twelve years as a member of our family, was left at the veterinarian's office with no ritual to celebrate his life. His bowl and leash just quietly disappeared.

Even today, I still hold a piece of that loss. And as the mother of three young boys I hope that some day their experience will be different. Watching my sons play with our golden retriever, Lucy, I witness moments of unconditional love, companionship, devoted trust, and forgiveness—qualities found in only the closest relationships.

The Jewish philosopher Martin Buber writes that, ultimately, all real life happens in relationship, when we mutually connect with another. For some children their relationship with a companion animal is one of their first such connections. Anyone who has experienced such a close relationship knows the possibility for rich blessings. In times of loss, it is fitting to offer a return of that blessing by honoring and remembering our companion animal's life.

Losing a companion animal is difficult no matter your age. Yet for children this experience can be even more painful. Often, children love more openly. Their feelings are less guarded, leaving them more vulnerable to being hurt. A companion animal has very likely been a member of the family for most of the child's life.

As parents, our natural response is to protect our children. But protecting them from the grieving process will certainly not make the hurt disappear and, in fact, can prolong it. Grief is an important part of healing. By standing beside our children in their loss—not trying to fill the absence, but just being present and available—we can offer loving support as they work through their feelings. The thoughtful activities in *Remembering My Pet* help adults guide their children on this journey toward healing.

Children make sense of their loss by retelling the story from their own perspective. Encouraging them to participate in the activities in this book, and incorporating their own words, will help them express what they're experiencing.

One day I will gather with my children to honor the life of our golden retriever, Lucy. I imagine that my sons' retellings of her life story will be filled with shared memories of the Valentine's Day we brought her home, her summers swimming for sticks at Priest Lake, and cuddling beside her with a good book. She has touched my children's lives, blessing them in many ways and teaching us all lessons in compassion, devoted love, and our connection with all of God's creation. Her death will certainly touch them as well. It will be part of our shared story. This book gives us some wonderful guidelines to help tell such stories.

As parents we cannot shield our children from grief. The story is there. But we can help shape how the story is remembered and retold. By seeking to honor both the life and the loss, it can become a story worth telling again and again.

What This Book Is about and How to Use It: A Message for Parents

If you have picked up this book, it means that your child has encountered death and grief, possibly for the first time, in the loss of their pet.

Death is a difficult transition for children and adults alike. We all have complex reactions to it. What is the meaning of life and its end here on earth? It can be intimidating to try to answer our children's questions—as well as face their confusion and sadness about illness, accidents, and death—when we are not certain of our own beliefs and feelings. How are we to protect our children and keep them feeling safe, while teaching them important lessons about the nature of the world and our place in it?

This book combines the wisdom of spirituality with the teachings of psychology to assist you in helping your child learn to grieve with less anxiety and more honesty. The activities in this book cover the various stages of grief and speak to the challenges your child may face following the death of a pet. Your child will be offered the opportunity to remember his or her relationship with their pet, and place this experience within the natural cycle of life and death that faces all of us.

In this book we address difficult concepts, including death, burial, heaven, and spirit, in ways that are open and accessible to children. The numerous activities presented in this workbook will help your child integrate these ideas creatively, by reading, writing, drawing pictures, asking questions, and making collages.

This book is best used when a parent and child initially look at it together. Your level of involvement with the projects will depend on the age and personal inclinations of your child. As your son or daughter works through the book, special moments in time open up for you to talk with your child about your own values, and the mysteries and miracles of life and death. Don't be afraid to have these amazing conversations, and to answer the tough questions, even if sometimes your truest answer may be, "I'm not sure." Take this opportunity, amidst your own grief, doubts, and questions, to grow in spiritual connectedness with your child.

We hope that the work you and your child will do in this book will help them as they travel through their lives, so that they can handle future losses and grief in a healthy and honest way. This hands-on book that you and your child create together will enrich your family in ways you can't yet imagine.

What This Book Is about and How to Use It:
A Message for Kids

If you are reading this book, something sad probably happened in your family.

Your pet died. He may have been a dog. She may have been a cat. He may have been a fish. Whatever kind of pet you had, you loved your pet and now your pet is gone. Although your pet was not a person, he or she was a member of your family. This book was written to help you remember and think about your pet who died.

This is your book. Unlike other books, you can write in this one. You can draw, doodle, take notes, tape in pictures, and even fold the pages.

 Begin by writing the name of your pet who died:

_____

You might be wondering what happens when someone or something dies. All living things have a beginning and an end. Flowers start out as small seeds, grow into big blooms with beautiful colors, and then they die. Little kittens are born, grow up into playful cats and, over time, grow old and die. God created the world this way.

All animals are born or hatched as baby animals. As they grow up, they learn to eat and drink and to get around by swimming or flying or hopping or walking on all fours. One day their bodies stop working, and they can't eat or drink, walk or swim, or even breathe. This is called dying. Dying can happen because animals get old and their bodies stop working. Sometimes, animals who aren't very old get sick and die of disease, like cancer. Or dying can happen suddenly, from an accident, like getting hit by a car.

However your pet died, you can have so many different feelings about it. You might be sad, angry, mixed-up, or scared. At times you may not feel anything at all. Your feelings might be going up and down like a roller coaster. One minute you want to cry, and then you just don't feel like crying. Some kids feel unexpected things, like wanting to act silly or to laugh a lot. Sometimes, kids feel guilty for things they did to their pets, or for feelings they had about their pets. Some kids might feel glad that their pets aren't sick anymore. Some kids are worried about their parents or grandparents, or about other pets they have, wondering if they will die now, too.

What are some of the ways you have been feeling?

_____

_____

_____

The purpose of this book is to help you during the whole year after your pet has died. You can fill out the pages in the order they're written, or you can skip around. There may be some pages you don't want to do at all. That's OK. It's up to you.

You may have a lot of questions about what happened, and about what's going to happen in the future. This book will help you to answer some of those questions and to encourage you to go to your mom or dad to ask more questions. You will become a "Memory Detective" as you piece together clues to remember your pet who died. As you fill in this book, you will be creating a special treasure that you can keep forever.

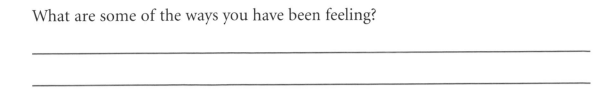

MEMORY DETECTIVE ACTIVITY

 Draw a picture of your pet who died. (You can draw from memory or use a photograph to help you.)

Let Me Tell You about My Pet

All kinds of animals can be pets. Many kids have cats or dogs as pets. Some kids have birds, fish, or turtles. Some people live in areas where they can have horses, chickens, or ducks as pets. Some kids have monkeys, snakes, or lizards as pets. Whatever kind of pet you had, this was your special pet.

 Write down the kind of animal you had here.

_____

Different animals live a long time or a short time. Bugs or butterflies may live for just a few hours or a few days. Fish might live for weeks or months. Cats, dogs, and horses often live for many years. Certain kinds of turtles can live for decades.

How old was your pet when he or she died?

_____

Pets come in all shapes and sizes. Some pets are as small as a chocolate bar, or the size of a box of cereal. Some pets are about the size of a basketball, or can be even bigger, like the size of a bicycle. Some pets are brown and black, or yellow and purple. Pets can have fur, feathers, or a hard shell.

What did your pet look like?

_____

_____

_____

Different pets eat different things. Some pets eat pet food that comes prepared for them in bags or cans. Other pets eat some of the same foods that people eat. And some pets eat pet food _and_ people food.

What did your pet like to eat? Who fed your pet?

_____

_____

_____

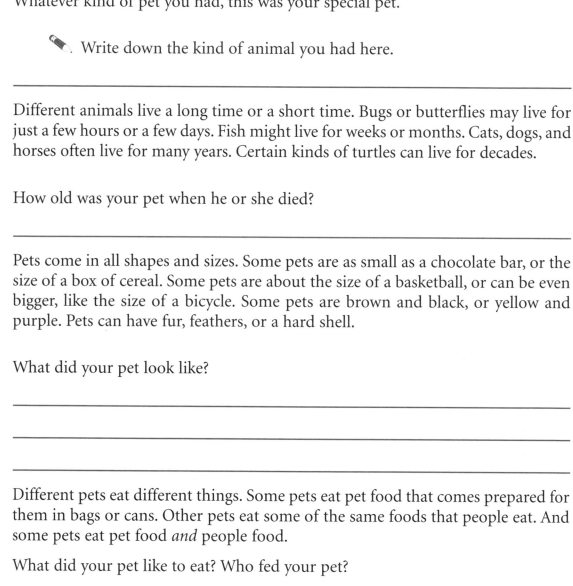

Some pets sleep outdoors. Other pets have a special place in the house where they sleep, maybe even their own pet bed. Some pets sleep in the bedroom with their owners, or even in their beds. Some pets, like fish and birds, often spend their time, awake and asleep, in their own aquarium or bird cage.

Where did your pet sleep?

_____

_____

_____

Did your pet make any noises or sounds? What did your pet sound like?

_____

_____

_____

_____

_____

"And God made all kinds of animals and all kinds of cattle, and all kinds of creeping things of the earth. And God saw that it was good."

—*Genesis 1:25*

My Pet's Name

Pets can have all kinds of names, just like people can. Sometimes when you get a pet he or she already has a name, and sometimes you or someone in your family gets to choose the name. Some pets have names that sound like the names of your friends, like Lucy, Cody, or Sam. Some pets have names that are usually for animals, like Flicker, Lucky, or Spot. And some people call their pets by names of things they love, like Cookie, Star, or Apple. Sometimes pet names are in English, but they can also be in other languages, like Gigi, which is French, or Kelev, which is Hebrew.

✎. Write your pet's name on the line below.

_____

How did your pet get his or her name? Who chose your pet's name? What does it mean?

_____

_____

Did your pet seem to know his or her name? What did your pet do when you called his or her name out loud?

_____

_____

🔍 MEMORY DETECTIVE ACTIVITY

✎. You can honor your pet's name by creating a name plate. Write your pet's name in fancy letters using crayons, colored markers, paint, or glitter. Complete the name plate by drawing a fancy border around your pet's name.

How My Pet Died

The first question some people may ask is, "How did your pet die?" They are curious to know what happened. Was your pet sick for a long time, or for a short time? Was he very old and just died one day? Did she die in an accident in the house or was she hit by a car? What happened? If you don't know the answer, you can ask your mom or dad. If you don't understand what happened, it is OK to keep asking questions until you understand what they are saying.

Maybe you heard that your pet was "put to sleep." This is not really about sleeping at all! Instead, this means that your pet was very sick, and maybe couldn't walk, eat, or play anymore. If the family notices that their pet can't do the things he or she used to and is in a lot of pain, they may bring the pet to visit a veterinarian, who is a doctor who cares for animals. If the veterinarian decides there is nothing that can be done to make the pet feel better, the veterinarian may suggest giving the pet a kind of medicine that makes their heart stop beating, so that they won't be in pain anymore. The animal may look like they are sleeping, but they are not. They are not alive anymore. When they are dead, they no longer feel any pain. It can feel scary to make the decision to put a very sick pet to sleep, but it is actually the kindest thing you can do when they are so sick and in so much pain.

Who told you that your pet died?

_____

What did they say?

_____

_____

When a pet you love dies, you may think about all sorts of things. You might wonder, "Who will die next?" You might worry about people you love or other pets you have dying in the future. What questions do you still have?

_____

_____

MEMORY DETECTIVE HINT

All of your questions are important! This is a good time to talk to your mom or dad about your worries and questions.

13

Pet Cemeteries

When a person dies, we need to decide what to do with their body. Sometimes the body is put in a special box and buried in a cemetery, which is a park that is just for that purpose. Sometimes the body is burned in a special fire, and turned into ashes; this is called *cremation*. The ashes can be buried in a cemetery or scattered in a favorite place that the person loved, like in the woods or near the ocean.

When a pet dies, we need to make the same kind of decision about what to do with their body. Sometimes a pet can be buried in your backyard. But other times that is not possible—if your town has laws against it, for example, or if you don't have a backyard. Your veterinarian may have suggestions for you, like offering to cremate your pet's body or telling you about a cemetery just for pets.

You can find pet cemeteries almost anywhere you go. If you visit one, you might see very tall gravestones and very short ones, gravestones shaped like doghouses, statues shaped like the animals that are buried there, and stone markers with all sorts of pet names and phrases carved into them.

There are even pet cemeteries on the Internet. In these cemeteries in cyberspace, you don't actually bury your pet's body, but you can put up pictures and stories about your pet whom you love and miss!

$\mathcal{P}$ MEMORY DETECTIVE HINT

You can see what a virtual pet cemetery looks like by visiting http://www.mycemetery.com/pet/.

Our Special Memorial Service

When a person dies, the family plans a service, called a *funeral*, at which friends and family come together to remember the person who died. Usually a priest, minister, rabbi, or imam leads the service, and someone may share stories called a *eulogy*, which means "good words," about the person who died.

After your pet dies, you can plan a memorial service for your pet. You can gather together the people who knew and loved your pet, like your mom and dad, your brothers and sisters, and even a friend or two. You can be together in your home, outside in your yard, or at a park. You can share stories about your pet—you might talk about what you did together that was fun, like playing catch, or share something very cute that your pet always did, like jumping up into your lap.

During the service, friends and family can talk about the happy times and the sad times you've shared with each other and with your pet who died. At the end of the service, each person who wants to can say good-bye to your pet, with words like, "Good-bye, Oreo. You were a great cat, and we will always love you and miss you!"

Some kids who felt close to their pets miss them so much, and aren't sure how to handle those feelings. They may cry a lot and worry that the crying will never stop. Other kids who loved their pets feel weird not feeling as sad as they think they should. Every person shows grief differently. There is not one way that is right or wrong. But for sure, even if you feel that you will never stop crying, a day will come when the tears will come to an end!

If you aren't sure what you would like to say at the memorial service for your pet, on the next page is a memorial service you can use (adapted from a service by Reverend Gloria S. Moncrief, as seen in *Blessing the Animals: Prayers and Ceremonies to Celebrate God's Creatures, Wild and Tame* [SkyLight Paths], edited by Lynn L. Caruso).

Memorial Service

Opening: We meet here today to give thanks for (*pet's name*). This creature of God was very special to the friends and family gathered here today. (*Pet's name*) died on (*date*) and we are here to mark his/her death by remembering the gift s/he was and the gifts s/he brought into our lives.

I would like to invite anyone who wants to, to share your memories of (*pet's name*) now.

Allow time for sharing.

Prayer (you can copy this so that everyone can say it together, or have just one person read it):

God of Life,

We are thankful for (*pet's name*), and for the time and the fun we had together. We are thankful that (*pet's name*) trusted us and loved us no matter what.

We give thanks for all the things s/he taught us, and for the ways s/he changed us.

We will always remember and love (*pet's name*). God, open your arms wide to receive one of your creatures, and we pray that his/her spirit will be safe with you. We are glad that for (*pet's name*), any pain is over, and the moment of death itself has passed. Hold us all together in the joy of our memories for years to come. Amen.

If your family is burying your pet, you can do that now. If you are not burying your pet, you can each put an object representing your pet, or some flowers, on the ground (if you are outside), or on a table or in a box (if you are inside your house).

A time for singing: Choose a song you know and like about animals and the natural world. Some examples include: "Rise and Shine," "Morning Has Broken," or the hymn "All Things Bright and Beautiful":

All things bright and beautiful,
All creatures great and small,
All things wise and wonderful,
The Lord God made them all.

Conclude the ceremony with a special prayer, like this one:

Dear God,

We are thankful for (*pet's name*).

We hold his/her memory lovingly in our hearts.

We give thanks for the lessons he/she taught us so patiently and lovingly.

We are grateful for the time we were together in this life.

As we grieve his/her death, we celebrate his/her life. Amen.

MEMORY DETECTIVE ACTIVITY

Write down a story you want to tell about your pet. These are your "good words."

_____

_____

_____

_____

_____

_____

_____

_____

_____

_____

_____

_____

_____

_____

_____

_____

_____

_____

_____

_____

_____

_____

_____

Pet Heaven

After your pet dies, you may have many questions. One of the first things you may wonder about: Where did the part of them that was so alive go?

There are a lot of different ideas about what happens to people after they die. Each of us has a body, with arms and legs and other parts you can see, and each of us also has a soul, which you cannot see. Many Christians, Jews, and Muslims believe that after the body dies, the soul goes to live with God in a beautiful place called heaven or paradise. Buddhists and Hindus believe that souls are put back into new bodies to have a new life. This is called *reincarnation*.

You may wonder if your pet had a soul, and what has happened to your pet's soul. Some people believe only humans have souls and go on to have a new kind of life after death. Others, who have felt as close to their pets as they have to any human, believe that animals have souls and go to heaven, just like people do. Some people imagine that the souls of animals and people are together in heaven, while others imagine a separate kind of heaven just for the souls of animals. Some people imagine that their pet's soul is reincarnated, and is born again in a new baby animal.

You may have your own feelings and ideas about what happens to people, and to pets, when they die. No one can tell you that you are wrong, because the kind of life any of us has after death is a mystery—nobody knows for sure. If it helps you to believe that your pet is in heaven, or that your pet now has a new, healthy body and a new, happy life, that might be God's own idea planted in your imagination!

Draw a picture of where you think your pet might be now: in heaven, on earth, or someplace else. What colors will you use? What kinds of things are there to do?

Making a Pet Memorial

After your pet dies, you might want to create a pet memorial as a special place to go to think about your pet. *Memorial* comes from the Latin word *memor,* which means "remembering," and it is a statue, stone, or some objects set up to remind us of someone who has died. Sometimes a person will buy a gravestone to put at the cemetery or in their yard as a pet memorial. A gravestone is a large rock with writing carved into it, usually with the name of the person or animal who died, and some other facts, like when they were born and when they died.

But you don't need to buy a gravestone to have a special place to remember your pet. You can make your very own pet memorial in your room, in a corner of your house, or in your yard, and leave it there as long as you like, with your parents' permission. You can set up a memorial for your pet with your own ideas, or work on it with your parents, brothers and sisters, and friends.

The first thing you need for your pet memorial is some kind of marker. If you are building the memorial indoors, you can use any kind of cardboard or paper. If you are building your memorial outdoors, you will need something more substantial, like wood or stone. You may choose to build a *cairn,* a small stack of flat stones, to mark the place. You might use nail polish to paint some of the stones with words, like "Twinkie, Beloved Rabbit," or designs, like paw prints. Your pet memorial might include fresh flowers or things that belonged to your pet: a favorite toy, a leash, a hamster cage, or a water bowl. If you want a memorial that will last longer, ask your parents if you can plant a tree, a bush, or some flowers in your yard. You could choose the plant to match your pet, like a dogwood tree for a loyal dog, or some catnip for a playful cat.

Design your pet memorial here on this page. You can then build the memorial either in your house, in your yard, or at the pet cemetery.

My First Memories

Maybe this was your first pet, and you got to choose it from a pet store or from a farm. Or maybe your animal came to you from a shelter for animals who need homes. Maybe your pet was part of your family before you were even born. Wherever your pet came from and whenever your pet came into your life, you have some special early memories. Remembering back to when you first met someone can make you feel happy even if they're not with you now. The questions in this section can help you remember early times with your pet.

If you were able to help choose your pet, how did you know this was the right pet for you?

_____

_____

Did you take care of your pet by yourself, or did you have help? Who helped you?

_____

_____

Did your pet eat special food or need special care the first few days or weeks? (For example, did you have to use a bottle to feed your pet?)

_____

_____

Was anything else important happening in your life when you got your pet, like starting school, or moving to a new house, or welcoming a new brother or sister?

_____

_____

_____

_____

Did you have any worries about being able to take care of your pet?

_____

_____

_____

_____

Did your pet ever get out of his or her cage or run out of the house without you? If so, how did you find him or her? How did you feel while your pet was gone?

_____

_____

_____

_____

Did you and your pet have any special things that you did together, that you both looked forward to every day?

_____

_____

MEMORY DETECTIVE HINT

Sometimes when we get a new pet they come with documents from the shelter or pet store. See if you can find any keepsakes, like papers or a photo related to getting your pet. You can tape them onto this page.

You can put keepsakes here.

What Other People Remember about My Pet

Your pet died, but your life will go on. You will still see your mom and dad, your brothers or sisters, grandparents, aunts, uncles, cousins, and friends.

They will want you to know that they care about you, and find out how you are feeling. They will want to comfort you and your family. They might want to talk about your pet who died.

You can do something important by asking people to tell you the stories they remember about your pet. These stories are like pieces of a big puzzle. When you put the pieces together, you will know more about your pet's spirit. *Spirit* is a word that describes what made your pet as special as he or she was, how your pet acted, who your pet loved, and what was inside your pet's heart. When you ask these questions, you become a *memory detective.*

Here are some questions that you might ask:

- How would you describe my pet?

- What do you remember about first meeting my pet?

- What was the most fun time you had with my pet?

- Did my pet do any special tricks for you?

You can record their responses on the pages that follow. This will become your Memory Detective Notebook.

 Memory Detective Notebook

Visitor's Name: ————————————————————————

Relationship: ——————————————————————————

What They Said: ————————————————————————

——

——

——

——

Memory Detective Notebook

Visitor's Name: _____

Relationship: _____

What They Said: _____

_____

_____

_____

_____

Visitor's Name: _____

Relationship: _____

What They Said: _____

_____

_____

_____

_____

Visitor's Name: _____

Relationship: _____

What They Said: _____

_____

_____

_____

_____

Memory Detective Notebook

Visitor's Name: ───────────────────────────

Relationship: ───────────────────────────

What They Said: ───────────────────────────

───────────────────────────

───────────────────────────

───────────────────────────

───────────────────────────

───────────────────────────

Visitor's Name: ───────────────────────────

Relationship: ───────────────────────────

What They Said: ───────────────────────────

───────────────────────────

───────────────────────────

───────────────────────────

───────────────────────────

───────────────────────────

Visitor's Name: ───────────────────────────

Relationship: ───────────────────────────

What They Said: ───────────────────────────

───────────────────────────

───────────────────────────

───────────────────────────

───────────────────────────

───────────────────────────

Memory Detective Notebook

Visitor's Name: _____

Relationship: _____

What They Said: _____

_____

_____

_____

_____

_____

Visitor's Name: _____

Relationship: _____

What They Said: _____

_____

_____

_____

_____

_____

Visitor's Name: _____

Relationship: _____

What They Said: _____

_____

_____

_____

_____

_____

"It's Just a Pet"

Sometimes you may want to talk to someone you know about your pet who died. It could be an adult or it could be another kid. It could be someone from your family or it could be a friend. You may hope that talking to them will make you feel better. But at some point, when you are talking, the person might say to you, "But it's just a pet who died, not a person."

Those words may upset or confuse you. You may not know what to say back to them. What do they mean? Of course your pet who died was an animal and not a human being. But a pet often feels like a member of your family. And you can love a pet as much as you love some people, including people in your family!

When someone says "It's just a pet," they are hoping to make you feel less upset. And maybe you do feel less upset. However, it could also make you feel more upset. It may seem like the person is telling you not to feel as sad as you are feeling.

People who say "It's just a pet" may not understand how grieving for a pet feels for you. Some people, adults and kids alike, feel uncomfortable thinking about death, or being around other people who are upset and grieving. You can try to ignore what they said. Or if you feel like it, you can say something like this to the "It's just a pet" speaker:

> "I know my pet who died is an animal. But I loved him/her very much, and this is my special time to be sad."

You can use these words, or words of your own that express your feelings.

✎ Write here how you felt and what you did or said when someone said to you, "It's just a pet."

_____

_____

_____

_____

_____

_____

MEMORY DETECTIVE ACTIVITY

Lots of people send cards to express how they feel at different times in life, like good wishes for birthdays or holiday celebrations. There are also cards to send during sad times, to offer love and comfort when someone dies. See if you can make a card to send to someone whose pet died. You can make the kind of card you wish someone would send to you. You can write the words, and draw a picture for the card. When you finish, you can tape the card on this page. You can use this card, or make another one, if someone you know has a pet who dies.

We hope that you will enjoy this book and find it useful in enriching your life.

Book title:

Your comments:

How you learned of this book: (check all that apply) ☐ SUBJECT ☐ AUTHOR ☐ ATTRACTIVE COVER
Reasons why you bought this book: ☐ RECOMMENDATION OF FRIEND ☐ RECOMMENDATION OF REVIEWER ☐ GIFT
☐ ATTRACTIVE INSIDE ☐ RECOMMENDATION OF FRIEND City   State

If purchased: Bookseller   City   State

Please send me a SkyLight Paths Publishing catalog. I am particularly interested in: (check all that apply)
1. ☐ Spirituality
2. ☐ Mysticism/Meditation
3. ☐ Philosophy/Theology
4. ☐ Spiritual Texts
5. ☐ Religious Traditions (Which ones?)
6. ☐ Children's Books
7. ☐ Prayer/Worship
8. ☐ (Other)

Name (PRINT)
Street   Phone
City   State   Zip
E-mail

Please send a SkyLight Paths Publishing catalog to my friend:
Name (PRINT)
Street   Phone
City   State   Zip

SKYLIGHT PATHS Publishing
Sunset Farm Offices, Rte. 4 • P.O. Box 237 • Woodstock, VT 05091 • Tel: (802) 457-4000 • Fax: (802) 457-4004

Memory Detective Mind Benders

With all you discovered about your pet in your detective work, try to complete the following sentences.

My best time with my pet was:

_____

_____

Having my pet die makes me think about:

_____

_____

I loved it when my pet:

_____

_____

Something new I found out about my pet since he/she died is:

_____

_____

Since my pet died, I sometimes worry about:

_____

_____

The one thing I wish my pet could do with me now is:

_____

_____

My pet taught me something about:

_____

_____

Photo Memories of My Pet

Photographs are wonderful ways to keep memories alive. When you see a photo, the picture helps you remember the people, places, and things at the time the photo was taken. You can create a special photo album on these pages. (If you don't have a photograph for one of these memories, you can draw a picture in its place.)

Photos you may want to include in your photo album:

- Picture of your pet when you first got him or her

- Favorite picture of you with your pet

- Pictures of your pet with your mom or dad, brothers, sisters, or friends

- Pictures of your pet in action, with special toys, or during special times like holidays

🔍 MEMORY DETECTIVE HINT

You can ask family friends and relatives to bring or send photos of your pet to you. You can also ask them to tell you the stories the pictures show.

My Photo Album

My Photo Album

My Photo Album

My Photo Album

Remembering by Giving

When we give something special from ourselves to someone in need, this is called giving charity. You can give money, or you can volunteer your time and energy to help someone.

The word *charity* comes from the Latin word *caritas,* which means both "caring" and "love." When we give charity to help the earth and its creatures, we are showing how much we care about them. When someone beloved dies, people sometimes give donations of money to charitable organizations. This helps keep their memory alive, even after the person is gone. You can do the same for your pet who died. And when you give charity, you will be giving twice: honoring your pet and helping the world!

Here are some organizations that help animals or teach people and animals how to help each other:

To protect both wild and domestic animals:
The Humane Society
    of the United States
2100 L St. NW
Washington, DC 20037
Phone: (202) 452-1100
www.hsus.org

To take care of pets that have been abandoned or abused:
American Society for the Prevention
    of Cruelty to Animals (ASPCA)
424 E. 92nd St.
New York, NY 10128-6804
Phone: (212) 876-7700, ext. 4516
www.aspca.org

To take care of wild places where birds live:
National Audubon Society
700 Broadway
New York, NY 10003
Phone: (212) 979-3000
www.audubon.org

To help poor families get oxen for farming, bees for honey, or other animals to help them survive:
Heifer International
1 World Ave.
Little Rock, AR 72202
Phone: (800) 422-0474
www.heifer.org

To train guide dogs to help blind people:
Guide Dogs for the Blind
POB 151200
San Rafael, CA 94915-1200
Phone: (800) 295-4050
www.guidedogs.com

To train dogs to help children with disabilities:
Loving Paws Assistance Dogs
POB 12005
Santa Rosa, CA 95406
Phone: (707) 569-7092
www.lovingpaws.com

Even if you don't have a lot of money, there are other ways to give charity that mean just as much. You can volunteer time at a local animal shelter, or offer to feed your neighbors' pets while they are away. You can clean up a local park or other places where animals live in the wild. Use your imagination!

Some Ideas of Activities You Can Do to Help Animals

- Walk dogs or feed pets for a neighbor.

- Help to clean kennels for your local animal shelter.

- Take care of a canister used to collect money for a local animal care group.

- Help out with office work at an animal hospital or zoo.

- Raise a companion animal who will go live with a disabled person when they are full grown.

- Take a family vacation to a national park service site and help them with animal-counting work.

Where did you choose to send your money or volunteer your time? How did it make you feel? Do you plan to go back to help again?

_____

_____

_____

_____

MEMORY DETECTIVE ACTIVITY

When you send money to an organization or do volunteer work, you can let them know that you are thinking about your pet who died. Usually the organization will send you a thank you note. You can put it on this page.

You can put a thank you note here.

My Life As a Pet: Pet Autobiography

An autobiography is the story someone writes about their own life. See if you can use your imagination and pretend that *you* are your pet. Write the story of your pet's life here, as though your pet were the one writing it! You can write all about your pet's life, or about something special that happened in the beginning, middle, or at the end of his or her life.

Remember, this is creative writing—it doesn't have to be 100 percent true. Maybe you imagine your pet had a secret life as a superhero, or could do things humans can do ... have fun!

_____

_____

_____

_____

_____

_____

_____

_____

_____

_____

_____

_____

_____

_____

_____

Grieving with Other Pets

Your pet who died may not have been your only pet. Lots of families have more than one cat or more than one dog or more than one fish. Or you might have a number of different kinds of pets living together with you, like dogs with hamsters, cats with guinea pigs, or turtles with parakeets. The possibilities are endless!

If you have other pets, they may be lonely or confused, too, because your pet died. They may have noticed that you are upset, and they may act a little differently in some way. Animals are very sensitive, and even if they don't speak our language, they may know when there are big changes, like death, in our lives.

You might consider sitting down with your other pets, explaining to them in your own words what happened to your pet who died. You can take them to the bed of the pet who is gone, or show them the empty feeding bowl. They may understand more than you can imagine! It's OK to cry with them, or let out any other feelings you have. It may even feel more comforting to talk or cry with them than with other kids or adults!

One thing you may notice is that your surviving pet's personality may change after a pet dies. For example, if you have two cats, when one is gone the other may take over the habits of the one who died, like becoming more cuddly, more "talkative," or more energetic and playful.

MEMORY DETECTIVE ACTIVITY

If you have other pets in your home, watch their activities for a day or two and then write down the ways that their behavior has changed since your pet died.

_____

_____

_____

_____

_____

If you have other pets, tape or draw a picture of yourself with them here.

Ten Great Things I Remember

One way to remember is to make a list. On this page, write down Ten Great Things you remember about your pet. You can include things your pet did with you (like playing ball or licking your face), the way your pet looked (big brown eyes, floppy ears, or bright red feathers), or how your pet played with other animals (wagging their tail or running in circles).

1. _____
   _____

2. _____
   _____

3. _____
   _____

4. _____
   _____

5. _____
   _____

6. _____
   _____

7. _____
   _____

8. _____
   _____

9. _____
   _____

10. _____
    _____

Pet Complaints Department

This part may be a little difficult to do. When someone we love dies, we usually think about all the terrific things we remember about them. However, all of us think about things we didn't like as well. Maybe it was a lot of work to take care of your pet—to have to get up early to walk them, to feed them, or to clean out their cage. Maybe you didn't like dealing with your pet's poop, or how your pet smelled. Maybe your pet had a bad habit that bothered you, like chewing on your belongings or making noises you didn't like. This is a page for you to be able to write out your complaints. If you want it to be private, you can fold the page over when you are finished.

Some things I didn't like about my pet:

_____

_____

_____

_____

_____

_____

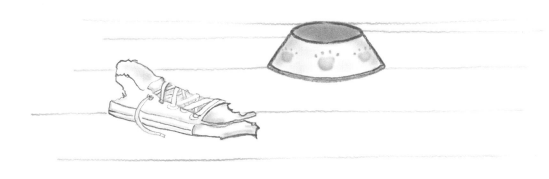

What about Another Pet?

Not everyone has the same feelings when someone they love dies. Some kids feel like they want a new pet right away after their pet dies. They may think that it will help them not to feel the sadness they are feeling in their hearts. Other kids can't imagine ever getting a new pet. They feel too upset to think about loving a new pet, or worry that they're not being loyal to their pet who died.

Mostly, it helps to wait a little while before making a decision about a new pet. Let some time pass, and you might be surprised by your feelings. You might still feel sad, or you might not feel sad at all anymore. Either one of these feelings can make you wonder: Is it time to love a new animal?

Do you feel a little guilty for wanting a new pet? You can never replace your pet who died, or the special relationship you had. But it's OK to want to feel close to a new pet. Wanting a new pet is actually a compliment to your pet who died. It means that having a pet in your life, with all the work and care it takes, was such a great experience that you'd like to do it again.

You might worry that if you get a new pet, that pet will just die, too. When your pet died, you learned that just like being born is part of life, so is dying. Every time we decide to love and care for someone, we know a time will come when we have to say goodbye, and that's scary—but the more love and friendship we put into our lives, the stronger we become.

If you feel ready for a new pet, what's the next step? You need to talk it over with your parents to see if they are ready to get a new pet for the family. If they are, you then have to decide what kind of pet you want. You might want to get the same kind of animal, because you had such good times with your pet who died. Or you might choose a different kind of friend, because you have grown and are different, too!

Are you (and your parents!) ready for a new pet? Would you like to leap with a lizard, or tango with a turtle? Do you want to play daredevil with a dog, or get a cat for the cuddles? Use the activity on the next page to help you dream about a new animal friend.

Take a couple of new pets for a spin by drawing three pictures of yourself, each with a different animal. Since you're not bringing them home for real, let your imagination run wild! How about a rhinoceros, a ladybug, or a gorilla? Try on some different pets and see how it feels.

You and Pet A:

You and Pet B:

You and Pet C:

Remembering My Pet
in the Circle of Life

This circle stands for the earth, which keeps turning around and around every day of the week, month after month, year after year. As time goes on, our feelings may also go around. Sometimes, memories that used to make us feel sad now bring us happiness.

Everything has its season, and there is a time for every thing ... be sad and a time to dance ... (Ecclesiastes 3:1–2, 4)

under the heavens. A time to be born and a time to die.... A time to cry and a time to laugh..... A time to

Inside this circle, you can make a collage celebrating your pet's life. You can draw, paint, cut out pictures or words from magazines, paste in photographs, pieces of ribbon, wrapping paper, or any other materials you can think of.

Glossary

Cairn: A tower of stones set up to mark a special place or show the way.

Cemetery: A park, often filled with trees and flowers, where either the bodies or the ashes of dead people or animals are buried.

Charity (*Caritas*): Helping someone either by volunteering or giving money.

Cremation: Turning the body of a dead person or animal into ashes, using a special fire.

Eulogy: Good words spoken about someone who died, usually at their funeral or memorial service.

Gravestone: A sign at a cemetery, usually made of stone, sometimes with pictures, that tells the name of the person buried there and also other information about them, like their birthday.

Grief: The feelings of sadness, anger, and missing someone terribly, usually after someone you love dies.

Heaven: A beautiful place without tears or pain, where some imagine that souls go to live with God after death.

Memorial: Something that is meant to help people remember a person or an event. It could be a statue, gravestone, painting, speech, or special ceremony.

Reincarnation: The belief that after death, souls are put into new bodies to have a new life.

Soul: The invisible, innermost part of a person that makes them themselves, and that some people believe stays alive even after the body dies.

Spirit: The special part of an animal or a person that makes them who they are; their life force.

Veterinarian: A doctor who takes care of animals.

Recommended Reading for Kids

Buscaglia, Leo. *The Fall of Freddy the Leaf.* Thorofare, NJ: Slack, 2002.

Mundy, Michaelene. *Sad Isn't Bad: A Good-Grief Guidebook for Kids Dealing with Loss.* Newry, Ireland: Abbey Press, 1998.

Rogers, Fred. *When Pets Die.* New York: Platt and Munk, 1975.

Rylant, Cynthia. *Cat Heaven.* New York: Blue Sky Press, 1997.

———. *Dog Heaven.* New York: Blue Sky Press, 1995.

Viorst, Judith. *The Tenth Good Thing about Barney.* New York: Aladdin, 1988.

Wilhelm, Hans. *I'll Always Love You.* New York: Dragonfly Books, 1988.

A Note to Kids Who Used This Book from the Authors Who Wrote It

We started creating this book, but you are the one who finished it! By working on this book, you have joined us to become one of its authors. It is different from any other book because YOU wrote it about you and your pet!

We wrote this book for kids like you, and we would love to hear from you about your feelings and ideas. We would enjoy seeing photocopies of how your pictures, prayers, and other creations turned out.

If you have some favorite pages from the book, we would be very happy if you would make copies and mail them to us at this address:

Nechama Liss-Levinson & Molly Phinney Baskette
c/o SkyLight Paths Publishing
P.O. Box 237
Woodstock, VT 05091

Other Resources for Parents on Spirituality and Animals

Blessing the Animals: Prayers and Ceremonies to Celebrate God's Creatures, Wild and Tame
Edited by Lynn L. Caruso
A compilation of prayers, poetry and blessings for and about animals, including memorial ceremonies.
5 x 7½, 256 pp, Hardcover
ISBN-13: 978-1-59473-145-7 **$19.99**

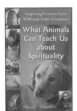

What Animals Can Teach Us about Spirituality: Inspiring Lessons from Wild and Tame Creatures
By Diana L. Guerrero
Ideal for readers who are interested in how animals touch the soul, and for those who have asked, "Do animals have souls?"
6 x 9, 176 pp, Quality PB
ISBN-13: 978-1-893361-84-3 **$16.95**

Other Spirituality and Grief Resources for Children

Remembering My Grandparent
A Kid's Own Grief Workbook in the Christian Tradition
By Nechama Liss-Levinson, PhD, and Rev. Molly Phinney Baskette, MDiv
Provides a sensitive and practical resource that will help kids ages 7–13 cope with the death of a loved one.
8 x 10, 48 pp, 2-color text, Hardcover
ISBN-13: 978-1-59473-212-6 **$16.99**

When a Grandparent Dies
A Kid's Own Remembering Workbook for Dealing with Shiva and the Year Beyond
By Nechama Liss-Levinson, PhD
Offers Jewish children ages 7–13 guided exercises, rituals and places to write and draw, list, create and express their feelings.
8 x 10, 48 pp, 2-color text, Hardcover
ISBN-13: 978-1-879045-44-6 **$15.95**
(A Jewish Lights book)

For Heaven's Sake
By Sandy Eisenberg Sasso;
Full-color illustrations by Kathryn Kunz Finney
After a grandparent dies, Isaiah seeks answers about heaven from people of different faiths and backgrounds and learns that heaven is often found in the places where you least expect it. For children ages 4 & up.
9 x 12, 32 pp, full-color illus., Hardcover
ISBN-13: 978-1-58023-054-4 **$16.95**
(A Jewish Lights book)

Spirituality for Children Ages 3–6

Does God Forgive Me?
August Gold;
Full-color photographs by Diane Hardy Waller
Encourages young readers to grant forgiveness and seek forgiveness from others in God's name.
10 x 8½, 32 pp, Full-color photo illustrations, Quality PB
ISBN-13: 978-1-59473-142-6 **$8.99**

Does God Ever Sleep?
Joan Sauro, CSJ
Helps young readers imagine God's role in bringing nighttime to the world around them.
10 x 8½, 32 pp, Full-color photo illustrations, Quality PB
ISBN-13: 978-1-59473-110-5 **$8.99**

Does God Hear My Prayer?
August Gold;
Full-color photographs by Diane Hardy Waller
Helps children learn how to communicate with God—without fantasy.
10 x 8½, 32 pp, Full-color photo illustrations, Quality PB
ISBN-13: 978-1-59473-102-0 **$8.99**

How Does God Listen?
Kay Lindahl;
Full-color photographs by Cynthia Maloney
Encourages children to use all of their senses to explore and develop a personal relationship with God.
10 x 8½, 32 pp, Full-color photo illustrations, Quality PB
ISBN-13: 978-1-59473-084-9 **$8.99**

Where Does God Live?
August Gold and Matthew J. Perlman
Explores the spiritual concept of God's presence with simple, practical examples children can relate to.
10 x 8½, 32 pp, Full-color photo illustrations, Quality PB
ISBN-13: 978-1-893361-39-3 **$8.99**